D0452187

IMAGINING ANCIENT WOMEN

IMAGINING
ANCIENT
WOMEN

ANNABEL LYON

THE UNIVERSITY OF ALBERTA PRESS

CLC
CANADIAN LITERATURE CENTRE
CENTRE DE LITTÉRATURE CANADIENNE

Published by

The University of Alberta Press
Ring House 2
Edmonton, Alberta, Canada T6G 2E1
www.uap.ualberta.ca

and

Canadian Literature Centre /
Centre de littérature canadienne
3–5 Humanities Centre
University of Alberta
Edmonton, Alberta, Canada T6G 2E5

Copyright © 2012 Annabel Lyon
Introduction Copyright © 2012
Curtis Gillespie

LIBRARY AND ARCHIVES CANADA
CATALOGUING IN PUBLICATION

Lyon, Annabel, 1971–
     Imagining ancient women /
Annabel Lyon.

(Henry Kreisel memorial lecture series)
Co-publishers: Canadian Literature Centre /
Centre de littérature canadienne.
Includes bibliographical references.
ISBN 978-0-88864-629-3

     1. Historical fiction—Authorship.
I. University of Alberta. Canadian Literature
Centre II. Title. III. Series: Henry Kreisel
lecture series

PN3377.5.H57L96 2012   808.3'81
C2012-900800-1

First edition, first printing, 2012.
Printed and bound in Canada by Houghton
Boston Printers, Saskatoon, Saskatchewan.
Copyediting by Peter Midgley.

All rights reserved. No part of this
publication may be produced, stored in a
retrieval system, or transmitted in any form
or by any means (electronic, mechanical,
photocopying, recording, or otherwise)
without prior written consent. Contact
the University of Alberta Press for further
details.

The University of Alberta Press is committed
to protecting our natural environment.
As part of our efforts, this book is printed
on Enviro Paper: it contains 100% post-
consumer recycled fibres and is acid- and
chlorine-free.

The Canadian Literature Centre
acknowledges the support of the Alberta
Foundation for the Arts for the Henry
Kreisel Lecture delivered by Annabel Lyon in
March 2011 at the University of Alberta.

The University of Alberta Press gratefully
acknowledges the support received for
its publishing program from The Canada
Council for the Arts. The University of
Alberta Press also gratefully acknowledges
the financial support of the Government
of Canada through the Canada Book
Fund (CBF) and the Government of
Alberta through the Alberta Multimedia
Development Fund (AMDF) for its
publishing activities.

FOREWORD

AUTHOR, University Professor and Officer of the Order
of Canada, Henry Kreisel was born in Vienna into a
Jewish family in 1922. Henry Kreisel left his homeland for
England in 1938 and was interned in Canada for eighteen
months during the Second World War. After studying at the
University of Toronto, he began teaching at the University
of Alberta in 1947, and served as Chair of English from
1961 until 1970. He served as Vice-President (Academic)
from 1970 to 1975, and was named University Professor in
1975, the highest scholarly award bestowed on its faculty
members by the University of Alberta. Professor Kreisel
was an inspiring and beloved teacher who taught genera-
tions of students to love literature and was one of the first
people to bring the experience of the immigrant to modern
Canadian literature. He died in Edmonton in 1991. His
works include two novels, *The Rich Man* (1948) and *The
Betrayal* (1964), and a collection of short stories, *The Almost
Meeting* (1981). His internment diary, alongside critical
essays on his writing, appears in *Another Country: Writings
By and About Henry Kreisel* (1985).

The Henry Kreisel Lecture Series is one the most cherished programs of the Canadian Literature Centre, which
was established in 2006 thanks to a leadership gift by
Edmonton's noted bibliophile, Dr. Eric Schloss. Delivered
by such prominent authors as Joseph Boyden, Wayne
Johnston, Dany Laferrière, Eden Robinson, Annabel Lyon,
and Lawrence Hill, these public lectures set out yearly to
honour Professor Kreisel's legacy, offering an open, inclu-
sive forum for critical thinking. They are part of the overall
mission of the CLC, which is to bring together and support wide-ranging communities of authors and readers,
and to facilitate groundbreaking research into Canadian
writings of any form, genre, language or region. The generosity of Professor Kreisel's teaching and his influence on
modern Canadian literature inspire the CLC in its public
and academic outreach and commitment to the remarkable
diversity and quality of writing in this country. The Centre
abides by his emphasis on the teaching and knowledge of
one's own literatures and of the world that informs and lies
beyond them.

——MARIE CARRIÈRE
Director, Canadian Literature Centre

LIMINAIRE

AUTEUR, professeur universitaire et Officier de l'Ordre du
Canada, Henry Kreisel est né à Vienne d'une famille juive en
1922. En 1938, il a quitté son pays natal pour l'Angleterre et
a été interné pendant dix-huit mois, au Canada, lors de la
Deuxième Guerre mondiale. Après ses études à l'Université
de Toronto, il devint professeur à l'Université de l'Alberta
en 1947, et à partir de 1961 jusqu'à 1970, il a dirigé le
département d'anglais. De 1970 à 1975, il a été vice-recteur
(universitaire), et a été nommé professeur hors rang en
1975, la plus haute distinction scientifique décernée par
l'Université de l'Alberta à un membre de son professorat.
Professeur adoré, il a transmis l'amour de la littérature à
plusieurs générations d'étudiants, et il a été parmi les pre-
miers écrivains modernes du Canada à aborder l'expérience
immigrante. Il est décédé à Edmonton en 1991. Son œuvre
comprend les romans, *The Rich Man* (1948) et *The Betrayal*
(1964), et un recueil de nouvelles intitulé, *The Almost Meeting*
(1981). Son journal d'internement, accompagné d'articles
critiques sur ses écrits, paraît dans *Another Country: Writings
By and About Henry Kreisel* (1985).

Les conférences Kreisel figurent parmi les programmes les plus chers du Centre de littérature canadienne, créé en 2006 grâce au don directeur du bibliophile illustre edmontonien, le docteur Eric Schloss. Données par d'éminents auteurs tels Joseph Boyden, Wayne Johnston, Dany Laferrière, Eden Robinson, Annabel Lyon et Lawrence Hill, ces conférences publiques se consacrent annuellement à perpétuer la mémoire du Professeur Kreisel, en offrant un forum ouvert et inclusif pour la pensée critique. Elles font partie de la mission globale du CLC, qui cherche à rassembler et appuyer des communautés variées d'auteurs et de lecteurs ainsi qu'à favoriser la recherche novatrice portant sur les écrits canadiens, quels qu'en soient la forme, le genre, la langue d'expression ou la région. La générosité de l'enseignement du Professeur Kreisel et son influence sur la littérature moderne du Canada inspirent le travail public et scientifique du CLC et son engagement à l'égard de la diversité et la qualité remarquables des écrits de ce pays. Le Centre prolonge l'importance qu'accordait Henry Kreisel à l'enseignement et la connaissance de ses littératures à soi et du monde qui les informe et les dépasse.

—MARIE CARRIÈRE
Directrice, Centre de littérature canadienne

INTRODUCTION

WELCOME to the 2011 Henry Kreisel Commemorative
Lecture. I'm pleased to have the opportunity to welcome
you to tonight's lecture, and to introduce you to our guest
speaker.

We are here, of course, to celebrate Annabel Lyon's
great talent, and to hear her deliver an original lecture on
Imagining Ancient Women. I first met Annabel when we
were teaching together at the Banff Centre for the Arts,
some seven or eight years ago. It was obvious from the
moment I met her, as it is to everyone who meets her, that
she is deeply intelligent yet blessed with the kind of self-
deprecating humility that ensures she will be embarrassed
by the manner in which I'm going to sing her praises.

Annabel was born in Ontario, for which we've long ago
forgiven her. She moved to British Columbia to get her
BA at Simon Fraser and her MFA in Creative Writing from
UBC. She is also a gifted pianist. She published her first
book, the story collection *Oxygen*, in 2000, and her second
book, *The Best Thing For You*, a set of novellas, in 2004.
The Golden Mean, her triumphant novel of Aristotle and

Alexander, was published in 2009. *The Golden Mean* was
the only book published that year nominated for all three of
Canada's major fiction prizes: the Giller Prize, the Governor
General's Award and the Rogers Writers' Trust Fiction
Prize, which was the one she ended up winning.

The Golden Mean has received so many accolades it's
hard to know where to start. I guess the best place to start
is to say that every accolade it has received has been well-
deserved. And it has been garnering attention not just in
Canada, but around the world. It has been translated into
French, both in Quebec and in France, into Spanish, into
Portuguese in Brazil and Portugal, into Croatian, Taiwanese,
Turkish, Finnish, Italian, Greek, Serbian, Hebrew, and Czech,
among others. When I last checked, her agent was in nego-
tiations to have a translation made available to the lost
tribes of Papua New Guinea.

But seriously, *The Golden Mean* is a luminously intelligent book detailing the intersection of two epic lives, that
of the philosopher Aristotle, and the boy/man who was his
student, Alexander, who would go on to become Alexander
the Great. The book is a masterful blend of the philosophical and the visceral, in which human beings are thinkers
and animals, tender and savage. It's full of gorgeous writing
that never once flinches from the truth of what man was in
Greece twenty-three hundred years ago. Under Annabel's
hand, Aristotle is brought to life so effortlessly in a first-
person voice that we feel as if we understand him, which is
quite a feat on Annabel's part, given that many historians
have said Aristotle was the last man to have known everything there was to know in his own time, although I believe
Stephen Harper has made similar claims. But through

Annabel's artistry Aristotle is seen not as a remote intellectual but as a man with needs, passions, jealousies, a man who wants to feel emotion but is overruled by reason, a man for whom we care a great deal. In Alexander, we are made painfully aware of the fulcrum between the life of the mind and the life of the body, the path of the soldier and the path of the thinker. To see these two men take the paths they do at the end is inevitable yet crushing.

The Golden Mean is, of course, the subject of raves worldwide. Here are some of the things critics and reviewers are saying.

Russell Banks wrote: "*The Golden Mean* is more than a brilliant and beautifully told novel: it's also a profound exploration of moral and philosophical issues that have troubled and perplexed us since Aristotle." Hilary Mantel, the Booker Prize winning author for *Wolf Hall*, her historical novel on Cromwell, wrote: "This quietly ambitious and beautifully achieved novel is one of the most convincing historical novels I have ever read."

To truly feel the accomplishment of *The Golden Mean* in your bones, however—and frankly, to feel it from all of Annabel's writing, since her earlier books are wonderful and should not be overlooked—you need to hear the language at work. I want to read a short section from *The Golden Mean*, just to get us in the mood and in case Annabel isn't reading from it herself. I could have opened this book at any page and plucked out a brilliant paragraph or an insightful interpretation, but I thought I'd read you a short paragraph, taken from when Aristotle goes to the slave market:

At a gem stall, watched by a bulge-bodied mer-
cenary hired to guard the place, I buy Pythias an
agate the size and coral colour of her baby finger-
nail, engraved with a Heracles the size of an ant. She
likes tiny things, rings and perfume bottles and trin-
kets she can keep in a carved sandalwood box I can
hold in the palm of my hand, a gift from Hermias.
A reaction against Macedonian ostentation, I sus-
pect: lately, the tinier, the better. The slave trade is
new to Pella, a small business still, catering to for-
eigners like me, and usually there isn't much on
offer. Today, though, we're in luck: a new shipment
is just in from Euboea. The slaver is genial, chatty,
smelling profit and taking his ease in anticipation of
it. He tells us about the journey, by ship, a rough one
with much sickness but no lives lost. He's got some
soldiers, Thracians, prisoners of war, good for farm
work but with a look in their eye that says they'd take
watching. He's got three young children, brothers
and sister, he says, and what hard heart would sep-
arate them? They're each eating a piece of bread
(a pretty show on the slaver's part), dirty but bright-
eyed, the girl maybe three, the older boy eight or
nine. What hard heart, indeed, though what a soft

heart would do with them is a question I'm not inter-

ested in answering today. (130)

In the end, the title of Annabel's book refers to one of
Aristotle's cherished concepts, that of the golden mean,
which Alexander himself, under Aristotle's teaching,
describes as the "point of balance" between two extremes.
Aristotle thought of it as the point of balance between
excess and deficiency, but to me it's beautifully animated
throughout the book, through the mind/body duality
Aristotle and Alexander grapple with, through the savagery
and harmony of Greek civilization in 350 BC, and even
through the present moment as a mean, though not always
golden, between the past and the future. Of course, the
golden mean is also a perfect metaphor for the quality of
the book Annabel has written, which interprets Aristotle's
towering intellect while revealing him as a flawed man,
through language that is both elegant and coarse, depend-
ing on what is needed at that moment, and through the
sheer scope of imagination that finds, amidst libraries of
material, the golden mean between what is necessary for us
to know and not to know in order to understand Aristotle
and his pupil as they shape the course of human history.
Cicero once described Aristotle's prose as a "river of gold."
How fitting that Aristotle has found a modern-day artist to
bring him to life all over again, a writer whose prose is itself
a river of gold for modern readers to swim in.

—CURTIS GILLESPIE

IMAGINING
ANCIENT
WOMEN

I thought then that to prepare to be "archived" is to go on an archaeological expedition, never quite sure of what one would find, often astonished about what one does find hidden behind doors one had thought were locked, with the key lost. Archives unlock the memory. Memory is ambiguous and ambivalent. We must remember, even if we don't always want to remember. Archives are our collective memory, and memory, however painful, is what makes us truly human.

—HENRY KREISEL,
from "Reflections on Being 'Archived'"

I WANT TO BEGIN by telling you the story of Philoctetes.

When the Greek hero Heracles was dying of poison administered by a vengeful centaur, he decided it would be less painful to be burned alive, and commanded his own funeral pyre to be built. No one would light the fire, though, except a warrior named Philoctetes. As thanks, Heracles gave Philoctetes his bow and quiver of arrows.

Philoctetes was one of many unsuccessful suitors for the hand of Helen, and as such was called upon by Menelaus to help recover her when she was taken to Troy. Philoctetes took Heracles's bow with him on the voyage, but was bitten in the foot by a snake when he accidentally strayed onto sacred ground. The resulting infected wound left him in constant pain, and its pus stank so horribly that Odysseus decided Philoctetes should be abandoned on the desert island of Lemnos rather than torment his companions with his suffering and his smell.

Ten years go by. The Greeks capture a seer named Helenus, the son of Priam, the Trojan king. Helenus foretells the Greeks will need the bow of Heracles to win the Trojan war, so Odysseus returns to Lemnos with Achilles's son, Neoptolemus.

Odysseus, knowing Philoctetes won't trust him after his abandonment a decade before, wants the noble young Neoptolemus to trick the injured man into giving up the bow of Heracles. Neoptolemus almost succeeds, to the point where he's holding the bow as Philoctetes experiences yet another unbearable spasm of pain in his foot and would be unable to prevent him taking it. But Neoptolemus can't bring himself to act dishonourably; in fact, he promises to take Philoctetes home, despite the awful smell of the wound. "A terrible compassion for this man has fallen upon me," Neoptolemus says, likening his own compassion to Neoptolemus's suffering. But Heracles, now a god, appears to them, telling Philoctetes that if he goes to Troy he will be cured, and the Greeks will win. Philoctetes obeys Heracles. His foot is healed and he kills many Trojans, including Paris, Helen's abductor.

This is the substance of Sophocles's now virtually-forgotten play, *Philoctetes*.

Aristotle, in his *Rhetoric*, claims that compassion is a painful emotion directed at another person's misfortune or suffering (Nussbaum, 306). There are three components to the Aristotelian conception of compassion: belief that the other's suffering is serious, not trivial; belief that the person doesn't deserve to suffer, that her suffering isn't her own fault; and belief that the person experiencing compassion is vulnerable to a similar kind of suffering. Put another way, this third element is an awareness of one's own frailty, a "there but for the grace of God go I" recognition. (We can dispute the validity of this third element—it does, after all, seem to root compassion in a kind of selfishness—but it's hard to dispute the emotional pull of imagining one's own vulnerability to suffering.)

Neoptolemus, in an Aristotelian account, experiences true compassion for Philoctetes (as Odysseus does not): he believes that Philoctetes's suffering is serious (the racking pain, the betrayal of friends, the decade of exile and lone-liness); he believes Philoctetes doesn't deserve to suffer (his trespass on sacred ground was, after all, an accident); and he recognizes his own capacity to suffer pain, betrayal, loneliness. Indeed, he goes so far as to echo the language of Philoctetes's suffering (using words like "terrible" and "befallen") when describing his own emotions. Clearly, he is as vulnerable to the sudden onset of unbearable, uncon-trollable, random suffering as his friend, and he knows it.

And what, you are probably wondering, has all this to do with the subject at hand, historical fiction; and, in partic-ular, historical fiction as it relates to women?

In her 2001 book *Upheavals of Thought: The Intelligence of Emotions*, the great American Classics scholar Martha Nussbaum writes:

Emotions...have a narrative structure. The under-standing of any single emotion is incomplete unless its narrative history is grasped and studied for the light it sheds on the present response. This already

suggests a central role for the arts in human self-
understanding: for narrative artworks of various
kinds (whether musical or visual or literary) give us
information about these emotion-histories that we
could not easily get otherwise. (236)

Later, Nussbaum continues:

The narratives to which we would naturally turn
or a development of compassion through the arts
are narratives of tragic predicaments, prominently
including classic tragic dramas themselves—for
example, the story of Philoctetes, who suffers terrible
suffering through no fault of his own. We can easily
see that such works of art promote compassion in
their audiences by inviting both empathy and the
judgment of similar possibilities. (351)

In other words, narrative works (and I would claim particularly literary works) are not merely helpful, but essential
to our understanding of the range of human emotions in
general, and compassion in particular. What I'm going to
argue is that literary fiction is uniquely poised to perform
an important ethical function in our lives—namely, to teach
us compassion, a deep and lasting understanding of the
other—and that historical fiction, with its particular tradi-
tion of focusing on moral problems and injustices, offers

a particularly interesting tool for performing that function. For the same reason, historical fiction also offers more pitfalls than contemporary fiction: it risks by its very nature greater didacticism, not to mention greater technical difficulties for the writer inherent in the creation of fictional prose that is hugely reliant on research. Anachronism is a constant worry for the writer of historical fiction. Or is it? In fact, ironically, I'll argue that for true ethical understanding—in order to feel true Aristotelian compassion with long-dead characters, and to gain real ethical insights thereby—writers must let go of the bugaboo of anachronism and embrace the present in the past.

Tools, functions, ethics, morals, irony: a dry approach to fiction, you might be thinking; martini-dry, dust-dry, dry as all academe. Enough to make a fiction-lover shudder. Where's pleasure in all this theory, you might be wondering? Especially the particular pleasures of historical fiction: the foods, the gowns, the jewels, the manners, the delicate dance of long-ago lovers who dared not express themselves freely, if at all, and whose passionate restraint made them far sexier than the easy lusts of today? In fact, I do think there's a place for these sorts of pleasures in the creation of historical fiction. No, let me correct that: such pleasures are essential to the project of literary historical fiction, so long as they don't make the writer lose sight of the essential goal of such narratives: to inspire compassion.

Let me begin by going into more detail about what I consider to be the main pitfalls of historical fiction. These are three: I'll call them easy moral outrage; forbidden love; and excessive decoration. Even otherwise admirable works of historical fiction can be subject to these flaws, and can lose some of their otherwise considerable power thereby. To illustrate each of these pitfalls—and how some writers of historical fiction succeed in avoiding them—I've chosen to give as examples not bad or formulaic works of historical fiction. We've all encountered too many of these, and there's nothing to be gained from criticizing an escapist bodice-ripper for everything it never aspired to be. Instead, I thought I'd talk about three extremely interesting and accomplished works that successfully avoid the pitfalls of these traditional tropes: Barry Unsworth's *Morality Play*, Lawrence Hill's *The Book of Negroes*, and Hilary Mantel's *Wolf Hall*.

First, let's look at what I'm calling "easy moral outrage." Nussbaum makes a powerful case for the anticipatory, forward-thinking power of tragic narratives, anticipating rather than rehashing moral problems:

[I]t is significant that [tragedies] tend, on the whole, to be in advance of their surrounding cultures in recognizing the similar humanity of different groups of vulnerable humans. Thus the highly hierarchical and misogynistic society of ancient Athens created tragedies involving subtle forms of sympathy for the sufferings of women; the slaveholding United States created Uncle Tom's Cabin; *the animal-exploiting society of Victorian England created* Black Beauty. *Tragic fictions promote extension of concern by*

linking the imagination powerfully to the adventures

of the distant life in question. (352)

It's worth noting, though, that these "exploitation narratives" are not strictly historical fiction. Euripides's *Trojan
Women*, for example, was written and first performed in
415 BCE in response to Athenian atrocities on the island of
Melos that same year. Harriet Beecher Stowe's *Uncle Tom's
Cabin* was published in serial form in 1851 in response to
the passage of the second *Fugitive Slave Act* of 1850. And
Anna Sewell's *Black Beauty* was written between 1871 and
1877, and set presumably in the 1860s (since one of the
horses remembers the 1854 Charge of the Light Brigade).
These works refer to their own times, not backwards; they
never set out to weave together the threads of present and
past, to show the relevance of the past to the present.

In fact, the tragic narratives of historical fiction—which
I'll define, very loosely, as fiction set before the writer's
own living memory—is almost inevitably playing a kind of
moral catch-up. We take it for granted that human history
is a history of moral development, moving slowly but inex-
orably forward toward ever-greater enlightenment. We've
come to understand that buying and selling human beings,
denying women the vote, making people of African descent
sit at the back of the bus, and forbidding military service to
gays and lesbians—to name just a few of the injustices our
species has perpetrated on itself over the centuries—are
stupid and wrong.

Of course, this progress hasn't gone unchecked, and
is obviously unfinished. Slavery persists in countries like

Mauritania, which didn't officially criminalize slavery until 2007. Human trafficking and sexual slavery exist in our own country. The mentally challenged and mentally ill largely remain objects of disgust and contempt in contemporary society. (Hard to imagine a film called *Black and Blacker*, or *Gay and Gayer*; but *Dumb and Dumber* barely raises an eyebrow.)

However, if we accept that the history of human ethical progress is more or less a vector, a cautious movement from ignorance and fear to ever-greater tolerance, then the first danger of historical fiction is clear. The historical novelist is more often than not setting her work at a more primitive time in our collective ethical evolution, and risks igniting outrage in the reader over an issue that is no longer active—or *as* active—in our collective imagination. It's much easier to get exercised about a settled issue than an unsettled one. It's fun and easy—but not especially challenging or intellectually engaging—to feel yourself on the right side of issues like misogyny, racism, classism, gay rights, and so on.

The American neuroscientist Dr. Robert Burton has gone so far as to show that moral outrage is actually pleasurable, even addictive; it produces a chemical reaction in the brain on a continuum with what we experience after a gambling or taking a hit of cocaine. (See his book *On Being Certain: Believing You Are Right Even When You're Not*; also CBC Radio's *Ideas*, "And The Moral of the Story Is...," Sept. 6, 2010, audio file archived on their website.)

And consider too what James Wood wrote in a *New Yorker* review ("Love, Iranian Style," June 29, 2009): "Sometimes, the soft literary citizens of liberal democracy long for prohibition. Coming up with anything to write about can be difficult when you are allowed to write about anything. A day in which the most arduous choice has been between 'grande' and 'tall' does not conduce to literary strenuousness."

So what's a historical novelist to do? We long to stand up and be counted on the right side of a meaty moral issue, to assert the greatness of our hearts and the tolerance of our souls. As the great American experimentalist Donald Barthelme succinctly put it, "Fiction after Joyce seems to have devoted itself to propaganda, to novels of social rela- tionships, to short stories constructed mousetrap-like to supply, at the finish, a tiny insight typically having to do with innocence violated, or to works written as vehicles for saying no! in thunder" (qtd in Louis Menand's "Saved from Drowning" in *The New Yorker*, February 23, 2009).

I'm not entirely cynical about this urge to take the easy moral high road. I do think our need for that hit of easy moral outrage—that pleasure in "saying no! in thunder"— is rooted in compassion. We wish we had been there to correct the wrongs of the past; we would have known what to do; we would have spared our fellow humans some of those centuries of suffering that resulted from what we, with the benefit of hindsight, can recognize as obvious wrongs.

Still, the historical novelist has got to find complexity even in the most apparently settled ethical issue or risk her story being so simplistic as to be not worth telling.

Let me turn now to the examples I mentioned earlier. First, Barry Unsworth's 1995 novel *Morality Play*. Set in fourteenth-century England, it tells the story of a theatre troupe who decide to re-enact a recent murder in a small town. Seeking to entertain, they begin to uncover clues as they research for their performance, eventually revealing a conspiracy involving paedophilia and the plague. The story is narrated by Nicholas Barber, a young monk who has abandoned the church to join the troupe.

Lawrence Hill's 2007 novel *The Book of Negroes* tells the life story of Aminata Diallo. Born in Bayo, West Africa, in 1745, she is kidnapped by slavers at the age of eleven and sold to plantation owner in South Carolina. Caught up in the turmoil of the American Revolution, she serves the British on the Loyalist side and eventually makes her way to Halifax and then, astonishingly, she follows the Atlantic slave route backwards, to Sierra Leone. Finally she ends up in London, working with the Abolitionist cause.

Finally, Hilary Mantel's 2009 novel, *Wolf Hall.* Set in Tudor England under the reign of Henry VIII, it tells of Thomas Cromwell, clerk to the King's chief advisor, Cardinal Wolsey, and later Wolsey's successor. Brutal, ambitious, and manipulative, Cromwell becomes the architect of the King's religious and political reforms.

The opportunities to take easy moral shots, in each of these novels, should be clear. Unsworth writes about a small-minded, class-ridden, ignorant, superstitious, and terrified society with no clear understanding of illness, moral guilt, and the connection between them. Hill's account of the horrors of slavery—from coffle to coffin, as it were, with rape, murder, kidnapping, disease, war, and much death along the way—is harrowing in the extreme. Mantel's Cromwell is a manipulative brute in a society that used and abused women in the name of religion.

But each writer finds a way to deepen the complexities of his or her narrative, and to find contemporary relevance in their long-dead characters. Unsworth's story has parallels in the fear, superstition, and paranoia surrounding the AIDS crisis of the 1980s. Hill troubles to make his characters troublingly complex: witness the sympathetic and conflicted duty inspector, Solomon Lindo, who buys Aminata from her brutal first owner. And Mantel, similarly, endows her characters with astounding complexity, making them utterly vivid to the contemporary reader.

Related to this idea of too-easy moral problems is the second standard trope of historical fiction: the story of forbidden love. It's easy to see how these are related. Love stories, particularly stories of sexual love, are the quickest way to scootch under a reader's defences and grab her by the emotional short hairs. We can't resist being interested in—and, usually, sympathizing with—young people in love. The subsequent supposedly moral complications— they're of the same sex, or different colour, or different class, or whatever—are revealed not to be complications at all, because how could true love ever really be wrong? And of course the thrill of secrecy and taboo that such romances entail—the stolen glances, letters, touches, kisses—become that much sexier for being dangerous, forbidden.

I argued that our predilection for easy moral outrage is rooted essentially in our natural urge toward compassion; we want to feel we could have helped, if only we had been around back then. Similarly, our pleasure in taboo love stories can be interpreted likewise: far from a trashy self-indulgence, I think it's rooted in our very human love of love. As babies we need it to survive; as adults we crave it for happiness and fulfillment. And sex is interesting, sex is fun. But as with easy moral outrage, the writer of literary historical fiction has to be very clear about the purpose of the story she's telling. Is the love story—all those rich descriptions of lace gowns and candlelight and stolen kisses—an end in itself, or does it serve the larger story the author is telling, the larger purpose of the genre: to inform us about the present via the past?

Again, let's look at how each of the authors I'm discussing avoid this cliché. Bluntly, they avoid it by avoiding it. None of these three novels features a love story as its spine (though each features love in many forms and manifestations). Curiously, for such densely populated works, each projects an aura of intense loneliness deriving from an intense focus on a single character: Barber, Aminata, Cromwell. By the end of each novel, the reader is intimately acquainted with each character's mind. We've gained intense insights thereby: not only have we become better acquainted with the world and time of those characters, but we've allowed the distance between their times and ours to shrink almost to irrelevance. Love is certainly one way of evoking what is timeless in our human souls, but these authors are canny enough to recognize that there are other equally valid routes: fear, honour, pain, intellect, ambition, compassion. By balancing the easiest and in many ways the most simplistic emotion—love, particularly erotic love—with these other more elusive and complex ones, these authors create fuller and more memorable portraits, and therefore wider channels back to historical understanding.

Finally, we come to the third trope of the historical novel: what I'm calling an excess of decoration. Goblets and

spinets and corsets, oh my! I can hear, from the devoted
reader of historical fiction, a certain amount of impatient
finger-drumming. I can't have moral outrage, I can't have
sexy love, and now I can't have the period stuff either—the
music, the perfume, the fabric, the food, the quirky words,
the idiomatic invective? What does that leave? Go on, go
back to your dry ethical theories and leave me alone with
my Philippa Gregory. I'm having fun here! I like gowns and
goblets! Zounds!

Let me respond by quoting two passages. Here is the
first, from Hilary Mantel's *Wolf Hall*:

> *He seems to be alone, but there is a dry scent in the
> room, a cinnamon warmth, that makes him think
> that the cardinal must be in the shadows, holding the
> pithed orange, packed with spices, that he always
> carried when he was among a press of people. The
> dead, for sure, would want to ward off the scent of
> the living; but what he can see, across the room, is
> not the cardinal's shadowy bulk, but a pale drifting
> oval that is the face of Thomas Cranmer. (274)*

This passage clearly turns historical detail to the service of the larger story. It is not description for the sake
of description; rather, it's description that enriches our
understanding of the characters involved. The detail of the
potpourri orange is used to twist the reader's understanding
of the scene—the man imagined to be holding it is dead,

and wants to "ward off the scent of the living," in a wonderfully revealing phrase. And note the tiny familiarity of that "for sure"—a fragment of language that is utterly familiar to the modern reader, slightly unexpected in the character's mouth, yet draws us closer to him and his understanding of the world. For sure, the dead wouldn't want to smell the living—a very specific personality indeed that can formulate this thought! The dry, dry humour, the evocation of a powerful, fastidious ghost, the shaft of insight into the dead man's mind on the part of the living man—Mantel turns that orange to good use.

Here is the second passage:

The palace, protected from behind by a mountain, faces north, with a view across the shrine and the city to the plain below. It's smaller than the palace at Pella but older and holier; all important ceremonies are held here. At the heart of the complex is a·square courtyard forested with columns; then reception rooms, shrines, living rooms. The circular throne-room has an inscription to Heracles in mosaic; elsewhere the floor is worked with stone vines and flowers so that it's like walking across meadows in bloom. Near the west wall is the outdoor theatre. A tall stone wall shelters courtiers on their way from the palace to the theatre, cutting them off from the public space of the city. The theatre is stone and beaten earth, with platforms for the audience and an

altar to Dionysus at the centre of the pit.

(The Golden Mean, *257*)

This passage of literary historical deadwood is from my own novel, *The Golden Mean*. It's the paragraph I loathe most in my entire book. It's dutiful description of setting, utterly bland and rote, offering little more than a list of archaeological remnants. There's no supervising personality to guide or playfully distort our understanding of place here, as there was in the "cinnamon warmth" of Mantel's room, above; it's description for the sake of description, the details numbingly accurate (the inscription to Heracles, the beaten earth) and utterly forgettable.

I've laid out everything I think historical *shouldn't* be; but where does that leave us? How to reinvigorate the genre, to give it the ethical significance I'm advocating without making it a dry exercise in didactic portraiture? I'd like to turn, now, to the process of creating a historical character, and how in my own historical fiction I've had to weigh the dangers of anachronism against virtues of hindsight.

My first novel, *The Golden Mean*, was set in fourth century BCE Macedon, and featured the seven-year relationship between the philosopher Aristotle and the teenage Alexander, who would go on to become Alexander the Great. It's written in the first person present tense, instead of the more traditional third person past. Instead of beginning the novel, "The rain fell in black cords, lashing his animals, his men, and his wife, Pythias, who last night lay with her legs spread while he took notes on the mouth of her sex, who wept silent tears of exhaustion, now, on this tenth day of their journey," I wrote: "The rain falls in black cords, lashing my animals, my men, and my wife, Pythias, who last night lay with her legs spread while I took notes on the mouth of her sex, who weeps silent tears of exhaustion, now, on this tenth day of our journey."

Now, quite apart from being a twenty-first-century Canadian woman of average IQ attempting to inhabit the mind of one of the great geniuses of all time, you'd probably think that I was setting myself up for problems by attempting to inhabit so intimately the mind and body of a person of the opposite sex. So let me begin by listing the problems I *didn't* when face writing about Aristotle.

I didn't believe—I don't believe—that difference of gender entails difference of intellect. I don't think through my breasts or my vagina, and I don't believe men think through their penises. The ability to grapple with the kinds of problems that engaged Aristotle—problems of logic, ethics, metaphysics, literary criticism, biology, politics, and so on—is not dictated by gender. (Aristotle, interestingly, would disagree. I'm not an apologist for his misogyny by any means, but I do think it was largely culturally dictated, and at any rate is a large topic for another time.)

Similarly, the physical differences between my sex and his never gave me a moment's pause. As a fiction writer, I can easily imagine being able to pee standing up, being able to lift heavy objects, and being sexually aroused by nice breasts. We've all come to understand, I think, that there's a continuum between genders, a fluidity, and that aggressive sexuality in women is as possible as passivity in men. Imagining myself in the sexual body of a man was a matter of imaginatively placing myself elsewhere on that continuum, just as imagining myself in the sexual body of another woman would be a matter of imaginatively placing myself elsewhere on that continuum.

I also have a husband to proofread for me.

The most interesting difficulty I didn't face when writing as a man was the matter of social difference. After all, male and female social roles 2,300 years ago were markedly different from what they are today. Women were considerably less than second-class citizens. They couldn't vote or own property; they were usually illiterate; they could expect to marry at the onset of menstruation and die in childbirth, usually in their teens or twenties. Middle- to upper-class women in Greece at the time I was writing about wore veils, required male accompaniment whenever they left the house, and were primarily occupied with child-care and weaving.

Contrast me, your average twenty-first-century Canadian woman. I vote. I own, with my husband, an apartment and a car. Obviously, I can read and write. I left my father's house while still single, though well after the onset of menstruation, to go to university. I started living with my common law husband in my thirties, and have two children with him without ever having taken formal vows. I've never worn a veil, even for dress-up. It's a matter of political principle for me not to ask a man's permission for anything. I can't sew, knit, crochet, embroider, darn, petit-point, tat, *or* weave. I *am* primarily occupied with childcare, and so is my husband. It's a job we share; a job we both love, and love to get away from when work calls. I've worked as a university teacher and a writer. I've run a marathon, slowly.

To an ancient Greek, I *am* a man.

Let me explain what I mean by that. I operate in my society with all the freedom that a man in the ancient world would have operated in his. Virtually every door that is open to a man in my society is open to me, and if I were to find one closed, I have a wealth of tools at my disposal—cultural, political, legal—to force it open. My three-year-old son knows about menstruation; my five-year-old daughter wants to be the Incredible Hulk for Halloween. Our understanding of gender and gender roles has changed so much since ancient times that I would argue they no longer correlate. A transparency of what it is to be a woman today would fit almost perfectly over a similar transparency of what is was to be a man back then.

Now, you might say, that's all very well for a first world woman living on the far left coast of one of the most liberal of liberal democracies on the planet. You might also say that I'm showing more than a little naïveté; that what is true in theory is not necessarily true in practice. Certainly, I can remember reading the stories of Alice Munro as a teenager and thinking, *All that oppression of women by men, all that unhappy marriage and resentful childrearing, that's surely ancient history; what has that to do with me?*, only to grow up to understand the truth and subtlety of her world that eluded me as a know-it-all teenager. And I understand too that there's more than a little of my own personality guiding my adamant belief in the equality of women.

I was a tomboy. I hated to wear skirts and dresses; my favourite toy was Space Lego; I never pierced my ears or wore makeup; I was fiercely competitive academically. I liked to read Hemingway and, later, Cormac McCarthy. I also grew up with an elder brother with Down syndrome. I mention this because I've come to believe that it accounts for a lot of my own behaviour in childhood, and the formation of many of my political opinions, particular with regard to gender roles and feminism. My brother needed help; he needed protection; he couldn't read very well; he needed someone to go with him when he left the house. Arguably, gender roles in my childhood were reversed: my sister and I were the strong ones, the ones encouraged to go out into the world, get educated, get jobs, learn to look after ourselves and the people around us; my brother was the weaker one, the one in need of protection, the one who was safest inside a warm, caring home. To an ancient Greek, my sister and I were the boys and my brother was the girl. I want to stress that my brother is not defined by his frailties, and in fact has many qualities—of empathy, of kindness, of gentleness, of respect, and of consideration—that I frequently wish on the population at large, male *and* female. But I can't deny that my unusual family life as a child contributed to my particularly forceful understanding of the world and my very entitled place in it.

Aristotle himself would probably have agreed with my analogy between the lives of the mentally disabled in our own time to the lives of women in ancient times. In his *History of Animals*, he writes:

> *[W]omen are more compassionate and more readily made to weep, more jealous and querulous, more fond of railing and more contentious. The female also is more subject to depression of spirits*

and despair than the male. She is also more shame-
less and false, more readily deceived, and more
mindful of injury, more watchful, more idle, and on
the whole less excitable than the male. On the con-
trary, the male is more ready to help, and, as it has
been said, more brave than the female. (231)

Mixed in with the misogyny are, I think, some grains of
truth. More compassionate, more subject to depression,
more readily deceived, more watchful: Aristotle makes
these observations as a biologist rather than a psychologist,
but I'd hazard a guess that anyone who's generally mocked
and oppressed—women back then, the mentally handi-
capped today—might well exhibit these characteristics.

I want to read you now a scene from *The Golden Mean*.
The female characters in this novel, you'll have guessed
by now, are few, and minor. This is a male novel featuring
male concerns and pursuits because that is the world,
frankly, I feel comfortable in. This scene features Aristotle
giving Alexander a lesson on Homer at a place called Mieza,
which is interrupted by the arrival of Alexander's mother,
Olympias, queen of Macedon, from the capital, Pella:

"I've read this already," Alexander says.

We're in Mieza, in the kitchen, seated beside each
other in front of the hearth. Not where I'd prefer to
be sharing books, but he's lately pulled something

*in his leg in games and has been told to sweat the
muscle until he can run on it again. He sits with his
heel propped on the bar where the pots hang, my
Homer in his lap. I'm anxious for the book—embers,
smuts—but so far he's shielding it nicely, taking
care. It's sweet to see.*

*"I know you have," I say. "You are Achilles,
your father is Peleus. Haephestion would be your
Patroclus, yes? Who's your Odysseus?"*

"Ptolemy. He's clever."

*He glances automatically toward the door at
the sound of bark-shouts from outside. I have him
alone today; his companions are out doing drills
as the leaves crisp and drift from the trees in the
high fall air. He's annoyed not to be with them. Hell,
he's annoyed not to be in Thrace with his father,
deposing kings, founding cities.*

"Do I have to go through it again?" he says.

*"You've read it with Lysimachus. You haven't read
it with me."*

*He starts to say something, then stops. I wonder
if Lysimachus has got his ear pressed to the door
even now. "Let's talk about book one, the argument,"*

I say. "Can you summarize it for me?" We'll see if
the prince considers this an exercise of memory or
attention.

"Nine years into the Trojan War." He's still staring
at the window. "Agamemnon has been allotted a
girl, Chryseis, as a battle-prize. Her father, a priest
of Apollo, offers a generous ransom for her return,
which Agamemnon refuses. Apollo comes down like
the nightfall—" here he hesitates, leaving a little
space for me to admire him; exercise of memory,
then; I say nothing "—and besieges the troops until
Agamemnon is forced to relent. But since he must
give up his own prize, he requires Achilles to hand
over his girl Briseis. Achilles, feeling the injustice of
this, refuses to fight until she is returned to him."

"Very good. And the squabbling ensues for the
next twenty-three books."

Now he looks at me.

"'Briseis of the lovely cheeks.' Do you suppose Achilles is in love with her? Or is his honour
slighted? Or is he petty and pompous and rather full
of himself?" I ask.

"Why not all of the above?" He shifts his leg
on the bar, winces. "I've noticed something about

you, Priam. You don't mind if I call you Priam? You remind me of him, the sad old king who doesn't fight and has to beg for his own son's shreds so he can give him a proper burial after he's been defeated. I've noticed you like to say, On the one hand—" he holds out an open hand "—on the other hand—" he holds out the other hand "—and then what we're looking for is some conflation of the two." He brings his hands together. "Don't you ever worry about being too tidy?"

"I don't worry about it. Isn't tidiness a virtue?"

"A woman's virtue."

"A soldier's, too. Tidiness is another name for dis-cipline. Let me put it this way. Do you think the story is a comedy or a tragedy?"

He holds out both hands again, juggling them up and down.

"Well, it has to be one or the other, doesn't it?" I say.

He shrugs.

"You didn't enjoy it at all?"

"Finally," he says. "Finally, a question where you haven't already planned the answer. I liked some of it. I liked the battles. I like Achilles. I wish I were taller."

"Men regress. It's a rule of nature. In Achilles' time, men were taller and stronger. Every generation shrinks back a little from greatness. We're just shadows of our ancestors."

He nods.

"You could read it as a comedy: the squabbling gods, the squabbling kings. The warriors running around whapping each other upside the head for nine years. Nine years! The farcical showdown between Paris and Menelaus. The trope of mistaken identity when Patroclus masquerades as Achilles. These are the elements of comedy, aren't they?"

"I laughed all the way through," he says.

"I know you have a sense of humour." I'm going to allude to Carolus's production of Euripides, to the head, but he's looking at me so brightly and expectantly, now, waiting for praise, that I falter. Such a needy little monster cub. Shall I continue to pose him riddles to make him a brighter monster, or shall I make him human?

"I've been working on a little treatise on literature, the literary arts. Tragedy, comedy, epic. Because I've been wondering, what's the point? What is the point of it all? Why not simply relate such history as has

*come down to us in a sober manner, not pretending
to fill in the gaps?"*

*He hikes his leg down from the bar and massages
the muscle for a moment. "I've been reading something. I brought it from the palace library. Wait."*

*He limps off, to his room I guess. Except he
doesn't limp, though he must want to. He takes
care to disguise the injury and walk evenly. A leader
must never reveal weakness in battle, in case he
demoralize his troops and encourage the enemy.
Something he figured out for himself, or had to be
taught? Something a king would teach a king; I hope
it comes from Philip.*

*He's back, breathless. He ran on it once he was
out of the room. The book he wants to show me is
one I know well, one of my old master's, where he
rails against the depraved influence of the arts on
decent society.*

*"Only, you know, he can't mean what he says."
Alexander sits again. "Because he uses theatre to
convey his arguments, doesn't he? A pretend dialogue between pretend people, with a setting and
so on. He needs the artifice for something, doesn't
he?"*

27

"Exactly. That's exactly right."

"To get the reader's attention. It's more fun to read than a dry treatise."

"It is that." I think of my own early attempts at the dialogue form. I had no gift for it, and gave it up. "Then, too, I think, you feel more when it's set up that way. You care more about the characters, about the outcomes of things. That's the point of the literary arts, surely. You can convey ideas in an accessible way, and in a way that makes the reader or the viewer feel what is being told rather than just hear it."

"Agreed." He's mocking me, but nicely.

"I too have been reading a book, wondering if it might interest you."

"It interests me."

I hand it to him.

"Small," he says.

"An afternoon's read at most. I hope it will amuse you. It's by the same author. The setting is a dinner party."

"Majesty, master." An attendant in the doorway looks stricken. "A visitor."

"Go away," Alexander says.

"Don't tell me to go away, you miserable little brat." Olympias brushes past the attendant, who jumps away from her as though scalded. "Kiss your mother." Olympias herself, all in white furs, silver stars in her hair, bringing in a fragrant cold breath of the outside. Alexander looks at her but doesn't get up. She bends to him and presses her cheek to his. "Lovely warm boy. I wrote you I was coming. Don't you read my letters? Don't lie to me. I know perfectly well no one was expecting me. That attendant looked like he'd seen a ghost. Hello, sir," she adds, to me. "What's the lesson?"

"Majesty, Homer. What an unexpected—"

"Not to me," Alexander says. "I've been waiting and waiting."

"Sweet." She helps herself to a chair and pulls it up to the hearth to make a threesome. "Well, sit down," she says to me. "Go on. I won't interrupt."

"Yes, you will," Alexander says.

"May I ask to what we owe this—?"

"You owe it to her majesty being bored out of her mind in Pella and missing her baby boy. I see little enough of him, and then that animal of a husband of

mine sends him out here. Dionysus himself blew on
my little pony's heels to speed my way. No, actually
I left all the servants outside. There's rather a lot of
us, and then quite a bit of luggage." Her eyes drift up
to the ceiling, perhaps the original of her son's man-
nerism. "I brought food," she murmurs.

"I love you," Alexander says.

"You had better. No one else does. Do you hear
from your father?"

"You're not allowed to ask me that, remember?"

She rolls her eyes. He rolls his, mocking her.
The whole performance is shocking: the anger, the
meanness, the grotesque intimacy, their willingness
to do it for an audience, me.

"Run away, now," mother says to son, as though
reading my mind. "I want a private moment with your
tutor. Go get them to fix me a room for the night."

He goes, taking all three books with him.

"We really did bring food. Rabbits and cakes and
things. I'll be terribly popular with the boys for an
hour and a half. What a horrible place."

"Yes," I say.

"How's he doing?"

"I think he's bored."

"Yes." She glances at the ceiling again. "Aren't we all. You will develop the existing faculties, though, I suppose?"

"Of course."

"Of course." She makes an ugly mouth, imitating me. "Does everyone hate me? We're not talking about Arrhidaeus. We're talking about my son. My son. The hell I will have to pay, when I get back, for coming out here without asking permission, just for a glimpse of my baby. Into the dispatches it will go: Olympias rode a horse. Lock her up! You know they'll do that. They'll lock me in my rooms. They've done it before. Last time it was for a month, because I went down to the parade ground to watch him drill. I just wanted to look at him, up on that great beast of his. I wore a veil but they knew it was me. They always know. Can't think how."

"Why did you come, Majesty?"

"I needed to see him. That animal thinks he can keep me in a box. He—"

"Mother." Alexander's in the doorway. "Why don't I give you my room? I can share with Hephaestion."

Olympias takes a swipe at her eyes with the hem of her cloak. "I would love that. Did I tell you I

brought food? Rabbits and cakes and things?" She
starts to cry. "Do you think they'll let me stay this
time? Just for one night?"

"This time?"

"She tried last month," Alexander says. "Antipater
caught up to her an hour out of Mieza. Why don't
you go lie down now, Mother? In case you have to
ride again tonight."

"You'll sit with me, though?" she says.

Noises from outside: a warning bell, men
shouting. Olympias begins to rock back and forth,
hugging herself and weeping.

"Go," I say. "I'll delay Antipater. An hour, anyway.
Both of you, go."

Alexander leads the way, allowing himself to limp
heavily now.

"You're hurt," Olympias says. "Oh, lean on me."

He takes her arm and they hobble out. Exit royalty.

(139–46)

Let me stress, again, that I wrote this scene from a male
point of view, from the outside rather than the inside. I
can portray Olympias's emotional distress as an observer,
but I have trouble imaginatively inhabiting it. To be perfectly honest, I can't imagine how every last ancient women

wasn't driven by the strictures in her life to suicidal depression, and that lack of imagination on my certainly coloured each female character in *The Golden Mean*. They're not a happy bunch.

Realistically, then, the life of an ancient woman is foreign to me, utterly foreign. Utterly, dangerously foreign, for a fiction writer; it's almost beyond my imagining. I can put myself into the mind of Aristotle with much greater ease, ironically, than I can put myself into the mind of his daughter. And yet that's precisely the problem I've set for myself in the sequel to *The Golden Mean*, the book I'm currently writing.

I realized very, very early on in my research into the ancient world that I had embarked on a two-book project. *The Golden Mean* is a male novel representing a male world: the public world of politics and warfare and intellectual ambition and the battle for influence. There are no major female characters in the novel, no conventional love story; I actually received a rejection from a foreign publisher on the grounds that the novel read as though it had been written by a man. (How, I wonder, do they reject male writers?) I always knew I wanted to write a companion piece that would look at the female side of this world: the world of slaves and kitchens and hearths, the domestic world, and also—in contrast to the cool rationalism of Aristotle—the religion, superstition, and magical practices that were traditionally associated with women.

After reading Aristotle's will, a fascinating historical document, I quickly settled for my female protagonist on Aristotle's daughter, named Pythias after her dead mother. Here's an excerpt from the will:

And when the girl shall be grown up she shall be given in marriage to Nicanor; but if anything happen to the girl (which heaven forbid and no such thing will happen) before her marriage, or when she is married but before there are children, Nicanor shall have full powers, both with regard to the child and with regard to everything else, to administer in a manner worthy both of himself and of us.

(Loeb Classical Library, translated by R.D. Hick)

Nicanor was Pythias's cousin, the daughter of Aristotle's dead sister, Arimneste. At the time of Aristotle's death, I calculate that Pythias would have been about sixteen, Nicanor in his mid-forties. Having been a sixteen-year-old girl, I know the prospect of marrying a forty-four-year-old would be unsettling, to say the least. I also imagine that a daughter of Aristotle would have a kind of double life: hard to picture that she wouldn't have at least a modicum of education, might even be literate, and (coming from the gene pool she does) was probably pretty bright; but, being a girl, she would also have had a foot in the world of women and slaves and kitchens, the world of magic and superstition.

Political circumstances at the end of Aristotle's life were—conveniently, happily, for a novelist—turbulent in the extreme. Alexander died in 323 BCE in Babylon of a stomach ailment at the age of thirty-two, leaving no clear heir. Immediately, Athenian sentiment turned against anyone or anything associated with Macedon. They saw the uncertainty and turmoil in the Macedonian leadership as an opportunity for them to get out from under Macedonian rule. Aristotle—born in the far north of Greece into the Macedonian empire, friend to Philip and his regent, Antipater (who was named as executor for Aristotle's will), tutor to Alexander—was associated with Macedonian rule at the highest level. Aristotle actually fled Athens, where he had been teaching for the previous dozen years, claiming he feared the Athenians would "sin twice against philosophy," the first sin being their murder of Socrates for corrupting the Athenian youth decades before. Thus fearing for his life, Aristotle fled to Chalcis, a Macedonian garrison town a day's walk north of Athens, where he had property inherited from his mother's family. He died there just a few months later, leaving Pythias and her younger brother orphaned.

Knowing Aristotle's last, best intentions for Pythias—a conventional marriage—I was curious what other options might be available for such a girl. Initially, I had planned the novel to be a chronicle of the last few months of Aristotle's life, a reckoning for him and a coming-to-terms for her: a gentle, subdued, autumnal project. However, once I began writing, I quickly realized that Pythias herself would have no opportunity to explore those options with her father alive, or so long as there was some other male relative around to take responsibility for her. For my imagination to really catch fire, I had to bump the old man off and take advantage of the unsettled political situation to send Pythias out into the world alone.

I also worried that the character who had so obsessed me in the writing of the first novel, so long as he was alive, would risk overshadowing his young daughter. His voice and emotional weather felt so strong and familiar to me, whereas Pythias—Little Pythias, she was in *The Golden Mean*, only four years old when that novel closed—remained hazy, unformed. Removing Aristotle would allow her to come into focus and speak more clearly in her own, distinct voice. Or so I hoped.

Accordingly, I rearranged my outline and moved Aristotle's death from the beginning of Act III to the beginning of Act I. The political upheaval of the time and the family's rapid evacuation to Chalcis meant the other responsible men in Pythias's life were either at war or left behind in Athens. After her father's death, she was left with a household of slaves and servants to manage, a little brother to care for, a farm to run, and a living to earn.

Back, now, to those options I hoped to present her with. The title of Sarah Pomeroy's classic 1975 study—*Goddesses, Whores, Wives, and Slaves: Women in Classical Antiquity*—provides a pretty good summary. Pomeroy writes:

> *The "glory of classical Athens" is a commonplace of the traditional approach to Greek history. The intellectual and artistic products of Athens were, admittedly, dazzling. But rarely has there been a wider discrepancy between the cultural rewards a society had to offer and women's participation in that culture. Did his wife Xanthippe ever hear Socrates' dialogues on beauty and truth? How many women actually read the histories of Herodotus and Thucidides? What did women do instead? (xiv)*

Pomeroy goes on to enumerate the activities of Athenian women at all levels of society: working in and around the house, childcare, cooking, making clothes. Wealthy women had "managerial" roles, requiring accounting skills; poorer women often worked independently outside the home, in roles that were natural extensions of their domestic duties: as cooks, vendors, weavers, midwives, and so on.

In May 2010, I went to Greece for the first time to research my Pythias novel. (I was unable to go there during the writing of *The Golden Mean* because I was either pregnant, nursing, or caring for my toddlers during much of the writing of that novel; utterly captive to my female body, ironically, while I was writing about the world of men.) I was fortunate to travel with a joint class from Carleton University and the University of Winnipeg, led by Professors Susan Downie and Pauline Ripat, with assistance from Professor Maria Liston from the University of Waterloo and the American School in Athens, and Professor Shane Hawkins, also of Carleton University. It's important to me to mention their names because their expertise and generosity were and continue to be absolutely unparalleled, and I owe them a debt of gratitude I can't begin to repay but by extolling their virtues as teachers, guides, and friends. I think Aristotle would have been proud to call them colleagues.

I knew the main settings for the new novel—Athens and Chalcis—as well as a few more specific locations that I wanted to visit, particularly Plato's Academy—shady and strewn with poppies, prompting one of my companions to wonder, if Alexander suffered PTSD and Aristotle was bipolar, perhaps Plato's contentment derived from

an opium habit—and Aristotle's Lyceum, hot and dry,
buzzing with insects, lined with a few small aqueducts, lit-
tered with the bleached shells of dead snails. We hit the
usual tourist destinations: the Parthenon, the Agora, the
National Archaeological Museum, Delphi, the Temple of
Poseidon at Sounion. We also visited the site of the battle of
Charionea, such a hot mess in my imagining, such a vast
and eerily quiet farmland in reality. We drove past the cross-
roads where Oedipus killed his father; there's a gas station
there now. And we got to experience angry Athenian crowds
in the flesh, during the violence and protests in response
to the Greek financial crisis. We returned to our hotel each
evening past broken glass, burnt-out buildings, and sponta-
neous sidewalk memorials to the dead.

Through it all, I took notes and pictures, asked ques-
tions, and tried not to think about the fact that I didn't really
know what I was looking for. Amidst the great marble edi-
fices, the golden masks, the temples and tombs and the
hillsides where the ancients met to practice democracy for
the first time, how was I to find one virtually anonymous
sixteen-year-old girl?

Images start to catch at my mind's eye; objects in
museums attracted me for being so unremarkable, so everyday, so practical, so unbeautiful. Cookware, makeup pots,
images of mothers and children. An ancient potty; a child's
sippy cup, complete with handle, spout, and strainer in the
top for mashing fruit. Crude carvings of midwives assisting
women in labour. Professor Ripat, passing behind me in
the museum where I found those little straining figures,
leaned down for a closer look and remarked casually that
they were probably carved by women, perhaps the midwives

themselves; men didn't usually attend births. Doors in
my mind started to open. In the National Archaeological
Museum I found everyday objects I'd never thought to asso-
ciate with the ancient world: lamp-stands, shelves, barrettes.
In the Agora museum, Professor Liston showed us bags of
ancient bones recovered from abandoned wells: tiny tibiae
and femurs, combinations of baby skeletons and the puppies buried with them to accompany them to the afterlife.
Midwives, she explained, probably dumped the little bodies
over long periods; some wells contained hundreds of tiny
skeletons. I felt the familiar prickle; there was something
there I could use. In the National Archaeological Museum,
I could hardly leave a case of surgical equipment—knives
and scalpels, ampoules, medicine pots, swabs, forceps,
a massive vaginal dilator. Professor Hawkins, he of the
twenty dead languages—how many of *your* friends read
Linear B?—puzzled out inscriptions, recommended books,
and gave me the gift of words—the ancient Greek word
for "fuck," an explanation of a name from Aristotle's will
that had perplexed me ("Myrmex," Little Ant), an appropriate Greek nickname for a girl named Pythias. Professor
Downie's hostility to the Macedonians became both a running joke on our tour and a precious source of insight. A
scholar specializing in the golden age of Athens, the fifth
century BCE, she grieved the loss of Athenian democracy
to Macedonian empire as I imagine an ancient Athenian
might have. Nevertheless, generously, she took care at every
stop to add a line or two about what happened in that place
under the Macedonians, for no one's benefit but mine.

I found myself looking outside the glass cases more and
more to the city itself. I took endless photographs of flowers

and insects—why? An outdoor weekend market, complete
with fake Rolexes, fresh fish, cheap T-shirts, beggar children, spices, pirated DVDs, and African immigrants selling
plastic tomatoes to tourists (you threw the tomatoes hard
at the sidewalk, where they splatted and then sucked themselves back into neat plastic tomato shapes again—splat,
splat, splat, the rhythms of these men's days, squatting on
the sidewalks, looking like despair itself)—these things
attracted me powerfully. Large feral dogs roamed the
streets, often accompanying our group for long periods,
alert, friendly, herding us; the city maintained a program of
spaying and inoculating them; the sidewalks were treach-
erous with their shit. By the end of our trip I had notes on
babies and puppies and midwives and ancient lingerie and
spiced meat; I had recordings of birdsong, and a camera
full of perversely obscure images—ancient BBQ tongs
and nail clippers and eyeliners and so on—I had only the
vaguest inkling how to use.

Goddesses, whores, wives, and slaves. Nervously,
hedging my bets, I decided I would offer Pythias not just
one, but every one of these options; she would try each in
turn, and carry forward what she learned from each "profession" into the next. She would study first to be a priestess,
looking for consolation in grief, and private calm amidst
external turbulence. I confess, too, the innate appeal of
giving her a priestess's power. Joan Breton Connelly, in her
book *Portrait of a Priestess: Women and Ritual in Ancient
Greece*, describes the priestesses "perquisites, honours, and
authority" as including, at the very highest level, "[f]reedom
from taxes, the right to own property, priority of access to
the Delphic oracle, guaranteed personal safety, and a

front-row seat in all competitions"; moreover, she could
pass these rights on to her descendants. Even lesser priestesses "enjoyed a wide range of benefits that derived directly
from their offices. Payment for cult services came in cash as
well as in skins and meat from animal victims, grains,
fruits, cakes, bread, wine, oil, and honey....By the
Hellenistic period—" my Pythias's period "—priestesses
received public honours that regularly included portrait
statues, gold crowns, and reserved seats in the theatre"
(197).

A nice life if you could get it, clearly; clear too are the
possibilities for abuses both venial and more serious. Since
I didn't want the novel to be a book about religion, I decided
she would become disillusioned with the priesthood and
move on. Next, she would turn to practicing as a midwife.
Here I would give her the opportunity to exploit what I
imagined might have been her father's teachings. Himself
the son of a physician, I imagine he might have passed
some of his own medical knowledge on to her along with
his medical tools. Midwifery, as Professor Ripat had pointed
out, was traditionally practiced by women, and I imagined
Pythias rejoicing in childbirth as did her grandfather in *The
Golden Mean*, as well as revelling in the opportunity to put
her education to practical use. Practically a child still herself, though, I also imagined her pity and terror in the face
of the many, many problems facing women in childbirth
in the ancient world, and the attendant dark duties of the
midwife, including the regular mercy-killing of babies not
expected to survive.

So she would move on again. Always with the momentum
of the narrative in the back of my mind, I knew I had to

keep raising the stakes for Pythias, making each stab at life more desperate—and more desperately necessary—than the last. I imagined her farm unprofitable, her money running out, her household falling apart. She is young, educated, cultured; and she has a teenage girl's curiosity about the life of the body. We are bipolar, these days, about teenage female sexuality. One the one hand, we idealize it in music videos and novels featuring vampires; sexuality means love. On the other hand, sexual activity amongst teenage girls is seen as something dark and dangerous or soulless and empty, a necessary narrative of abuse and victimization. But as surely and as paradoxically as we link sex with love on the one hand and abuse on the other, the truth must be something more muddled, deeper and richer and infinitely more complex. I wanted Pythias's sexual life—for she'll now move on to the profession of *hetaira*, or courtesan—to be, borrowing the Metaphysical poet Henry Vaughan's phrase, "a deep, but dazzling darkness" ("The Night").

Two brilliant and oddly divergent books have contributed my understanding of this complexity. The first was Padma Viswanathan's 2008 novel *The Toss of a Lemon*. A multi-generational story spanning many decades of twentieth-century India, this novel at first glance has little to do with the sex life of a teenage girl in ancient Greece. What fascinated me about this novel, though, was its utterly believable portrait of an arranged marriage. Arranged marriages are one of those conventions historical fictions love to thwart; comic heroines are forever escaping them; tragic heroines are forever being miserably trapped by them. But Viswanathan does something much more subtle and interesting. She

portrays an intelligent, sympathetic, traditional young
woman who goes through with an arranged marriage and
finds a complex life on the other side: not comic, not tragic,
but rich and complicated, where man and woman learn
to care for each other after, rather than before, marriage.
Arranged marriage was of course commonplace in ancient
Greece, as it is in much of the world today; rather than
taking a first-world Westerner's black-and-white approach
to the practice, this novel taught me to consider it with
more maturity and subtlety, for what it can offer as well as
what it takes away.

In many ways, Amber Dawn's 2010 novel *Sub Rosa*
could not provide more of a contrast. This fantastical novel
features a teenage prostitute named Little who gets lured
into a world that is simultaneously a teenager's dream and
nightmare—a world of sparkly clothes and makeovers and
sweet food and doting men, whose sexual appetites she
must serve. She becomes a so-called "Glory," a prostitute
of exceptional beauty and ability and solace, with all the
attendant status in her society. Escape becomes one of the
central themes of the novel: paradoxically, though, Dawn
looks at escape through both sides of the looking glass:
escape *to* the world of prostitution as well as escape *from* it.
She captures the conflicted mind of the teenage girl with
astute insights, as well as frankly acknowledging the complexities of teenage sexuality.

An ancient Athenian would have understood the concept
of the "Glory." Pomeroy writes that, in the ancient world,
prostitution was stratified just as the rest of society was. At
bottom were prostitutes who were slaves; at the top were
the *hetairai*, the "companions to men." She writes, "Many

of these, in addition to physical beauty, had had intellectual training and possessed artistic talents, attributes that made them more entertaining companions to Athenian men at parties than their legitimate wives. It is no accident that the most famous woman in fifth-century Athens was the foreign-born Aspasia" (89), companion of Pericles, friend of Socrates. Pomeroy goes on to note that prostitutes were "the only women in Athens who exercised independent control over considerable amounts of money" (91).

Power, again: I wanted to find a way to give Pythias power, to give her the resources to act as a man in a world of men. Was this an exercise in anachronism, or an attempt to bring her closer to me, to understand her in the only way I could? Both?

It was tempting to give her the independent, wealthy, cultured life of an Aspasia and leave it at that: a happy ending or sorts, a chance to be more than just—as Pomeroy wryly remarks in her preface—one of those "creatures who bleed and breed" (xii). But wars end, and men come home, and I couldn't resist offering her a final act.

For finally, of course, we come to marriage and motherhood. For a long time, I wanted to ignore this option. How parochial, how dull; how too, too like my own life! What had I been attempting all this time, after all, if not to spare her the conventional and offer her power, excitement, choices?

It's appropriate, here, to revisit the sins of historical fiction I listed at the outset: anachronism, forbidden love, excessive description. Perhaps all three of these are subsets of the greatest sin of all that a historical novelist can commit: that of escapism.

As a reader—and as a writer—I confess no small part of my pleasure is in escaping my everyday world. A little sketch of that world: I live in New Westminster, British Columbia, a tough, grey suburb of one of the rainiest cities in the world, Vancouver. The beauties of Vancouver—the mountains, the ocean—are not usually visible to me. I get up with the kids, dress them for the rain, get them to school, go to Safeway, eke out an hour or two of work, usually in a coffee shop because my husband works nights and needs to sleep; then pick the kids up and spend the rest of the day seeing to their needs until bedtime, when I try to eke out another hour or so before my brain gives out.

Now, don't get me wrong: it's a good life, the life I've chosen. I love my family and my city; I like rain and mist and green and grey; I've even gotten used to working in coffee shops. But without books and reading and the wider world they offer, I get short-tempered, irritable; I lose my patience and my compassion, my ability to function kindly in the world. I need not only to be able to imagine myself in a different mind and body at a different time; I need to feel my own life enriched thereby. I need to see the links between what I'm reading to my own life, otherwise the pleasure in that experience, paradoxically, becomes a sterile intellectual exercise without richness or depth. Historical fiction has to be more than just Halloween for grown-ups, putting on a costume for a night, for it to be truly satisfying and significant; an achievement of humanity rather than just an achievement of research.

In other words, it's necessary to confront the probable, the real, both in my own life and in the lives of my characters. By offering my characters the escape afforded

by anachronistic possibilities—such as offering Pythias
nothing but power in a society where that was utterly
unlikely—offering her my own experience of the world—
I'm denying both the reality of her world, and refusing
to enrich my own by forcing myself outside of my own
experience.

Marriage, then; and to precisely the man her father chose
for her. What could be more prosaic, more disappointing,
but—crucially—more probable? Most ancient women
had their marriages arranged for them; why does Pythias
become less interesting if I imagine her conforming rather
than rebelling? The truth is that she only becomes less
interesting if I make her so; it's my job as writer to show
the richness in the mundane.

So how; how? Back to my original problem in dealing
with ancient women: their lives appall me; I can't imagine
their lives; I don't want to; I don't know where to begin.

But of course that's wrong: every woman knows where to
begin. Marriage, childbirth, motherhood: these are touch-
stones, things that haven't essentially changed (give or take
an epidural or two) over the millennia. Love, desire, pain,
motherhood, the body: these endure. I could reach back to
her experience of the world by drawing, most intimately,
upon my own: my experience of touching a male body sexually for the first time; my experience of childbirth; my
experience of running a household on a tight budget; my
experience of the trials and consolations of marriage—these
things aren't dreadfully or shamefully dull or boring, dis-
gustingly unworthy of art. Martha Nussbaum writes that
tragic narratives help the viewer to contemplate what is
awful and hideous and dull and shameful in life with

compassion and recognition of those elements in her *own* life. She evokes the story of Philoctetes, reminding us that Neoptolemus wasn't scared away by the stench of Philoctetes's wound, but rather he was drawn closer by the plight of his suffering friend. She writes:

> *So too with the spectator: she finds herself looking unabashed at an outcast who was left alone because he was apparently intolerable to be with. And she is made fully aware that in so befriending Philoctetes she is befriending those elements of his life that belong to her own as well. In fact, she befriends herself.* (352)

Let's return to the story I told you at the outset, the story of Philoctetes. Let's imagine it a little differently. Let's pretend that Philoctetes is a woman, a girl, left alone by political turbulence and death. Let's pretend that her festering wound, the thing that makes her shameful and intolerable to the average reader of historical fiction, worthy of banishment to some remote island in our imaginations where we don't have to think about her, is her absolute normality and familiarity. She's not ugly, not beautiful, not stupid, not brilliant. She has no great artistic or scientific or technical or paranormal talent. She'll probably marry someone she neither loves nor hates, bear children, perhaps die in childbirth, perhaps survive. She is, in fact, the self the historical fiction reader must befriend, "thereby befriending those elements of the character's life that belong to her own as well." She is our modern self rediscovered in the past; the ultimate other brought home to us.

Incidentally, I'm not the only writer to play with the idea of Philoctetes. A quick Wikipedia search reveals plays based on that character by André Gide, Heiner Müller, and Seamus Heaney; an essay by Edmund Wilson; and poetry by William Wordsworth, Yannis Ritsos, Derek Walcott, Adrienne Rich, and Michael Ondaatje.

From Ondaatje's poem "Philoctetes on the island":

With wind the rain wheels like a circus hoof,

aims at my eyes, rakes out the smell of animals

of stone moss, cleans me.

Branches fall like nightmares in the dark

till sun breaks up

and spreads wound fire at my feet

then they smell me,

the beautiful animals

—*from* Rat Jelly *(35)*

This poem provides a neat link to my final topic, that of language; specifically, the use of contemporary language to illuminate a long-gone world. Ondaatje tells an ancient tale in rigorously modern diction; witness the almost cubist use of language to convey Philoctetes's agony, the way words and images are brutally, jaggedly juxtaposed. This choice gives the poem its immediacy and power. Had Ondaatje instead chosen a diction that merely mimicked that of Sophocles, say, I suspect Philoctetes's pain wouldn't have been so vivid to the reader as it is here; the reader might have admired the technical job of mimicry without feeling viscerally Philoctetes's pain, and relating it to her own body and life thereby.

For similar reasons, in *The Golden Mean* I chose to use a lot of contemporary, borderline anachronistic language. The characters curse like twenty-first-century Canadians, speak in sentence fragments, stammer, use sarcasm, and make jokes. I didn't want to write a historical novel; rather, I wanted to write a contemporary novel that happened to be set twenty-three hundred years ago. I wanted the reader to feel as though she could be in the room with my characters, have conversations with them. I took care to sand smooth any patches of historical filigree that might have distracted the reader from the immediacy of the characters, using "dress" instead of "chiton," for instance, and referring to Alexander's horse—"horse," mind you, not "mount" or "charger"—not as the legendary "Bucephalus," but rather as the less familiar "Oxhead."

One of the unexpected consequences of this use of modern language, for me, was the attendant transition to comedy. Where this expressed itself as a certain dark humour in *The Golden Mean*, I'm finding it's becoming more insidious, or more profound, in the new novel, informing not just the character's speech or personalities, but actually manifesting itself in the novel's theme. I want Pythias, for all her trials and tribulations, to be a comic heroine. As you'll have gathered from everything I've said so far tonight, I revere the work of Martha Nussbaum. Her influence on my life—not just my intellectual life, but my choice of career—has been profound. I began as a student of philosophy and then turned to law; but reading her work—particularly *The Fragility of Goodness: Luck and Ethics in Greek Tragedy and Philosophy* and *Love's Knowledge: Essays on Philosophy and Literature*—persuaded me that I could pursue my intellectual interests, particularly in ethics, through fiction; I quit law school to become a fiction writer, and have never looked back.

However, I find myself beginning to differ with Nussbaum on one major point. She writes: "[I]f the arts in general make human vulnerability pleasing, tragic dramas (and other works describing tragic plights) encourage pleasure of the most difficult type: the pleasure of contemplating our mortality and our vulnerability to the worst disasters in life" (Nussbaum, 352). Now, I don't deny that this is so; but I'm beginning to wonder if it's too narrow a conception of the possibilities of the literary arts. Could we not "contemplate our mortality and our vulnerability to the worst disasters in life" via comedy? I have no illusions about my own originality here: in *The Tempest, Don Quixote,* and *Barney's Version*—to take three examples off the very top of my head—Shakespeare, Cervantes, and Mordecai Richler are there well before me. But I do think it's worth reminding ourselves, *particularly* in the context of historical fiction, that comedy is an option. Too often, hamstrung by the ethical plights facing our characters, we writers respond with violence, misery, tragic misunderstanding, and mortal po-facedness. We corset our characters' speech as minutely as their bodies (in all that period-perfect, exhaustively researched underwear), and fail to notice their humanity slipping out the door. I believe it's not only desirable but utterly necessary to *inhabit* the past rather than simply portray it; and if the risk is anachronism, that's a risk that this historical novelist is willing to take.

I still have worries; what writer doesn't? I worry I've still been too kind to Pythias: she's young, healthy, utterly middle-class. I haven't yet built into my outline the possibility of making her a slave; perhaps that's something I need to rethink. Nor have I really taken into account the utter squalor and stench and grubbiness of the ancient world: the bad breath and body odour and snaggle-teeth and infections and deformities and chamber pots and menstrual rags and dirty food and—well, you get the picture. I have, perhaps, not yet pushed myself far enough in the direction of my own arguments: that the historical novelist should—must—err on the side of over-familiarity, treating her characters as women you might meet in contemporary Canada rather than unreachable aliens, if her work is to have the contemporary relevance and resonance essential to the best fiction. She is my Philoctetes, the creature who both repels and inspires compassion, the ancient self I can choose to befriend, and enrich my own modern life thereby.

WORKS CITED

Aristotle. *Aristotle's History of Animals.* Trans. Richard Cresswell.
     Book IX. London: Henry G. Bohm, 1862.

Connelly, Joan Breton. *Portrait of a Priestess: Women and Ritual in
     Ancient Greece.* Princeton: Princeton University Press, 2007.

Diogenes Laertius. *Lives of Eminent Philosophers.* Trans. R.D. Hicks.
     Vol. 1. Cambridge, MA: Harvard University Press, 1925. Loeb
     Classic Library Ser. 184.

Kreisel, Henry. "Reflections on Being 'Archived'." *Canadian
     Literature,* 8 Dec. 2011. Web. 24 Jan. 2012.

Lyon, Annabel. *The Golden Mean.* Toronto: Random House
     Canada, 2009.

Mantel, Hilary. *Wolf Hall.* Toronto: HarperCollins Canada, 2009.

Nussbaum, Martha C. *Upheavals of Thought: The Intelligence of
     Emotions.* Cambridge: Cambridge University Press, 2001.

Ondaatje, Michael. "Philoctetes on the island." In *Rat Jelly.*
     Toronto: Coach House Press, 1973. 34–35.

Pomeroy, Sarah B. *Goddesses, Whores, Wives, and Slaves: Women in
     Classical Antiquity.* New York: Schocken Books, 1975.

Vaughan, Henry. "The Night." *The Poems of Henry Vaughan,
     Silurist.* Vol I. E.K. Chambers, Ed. London: Lawrence & Bullen,
     1896. 253.

HENRY KREISEL LECTURE SERIES

From Mushkegowuk to New Orleans
A Mixed Blood Highway
JOSEPH BOYDEN
ISBN 978–1–897126–29–5

The Old Lost Land of Newfoundland
Family, Memory, Fiction, and Myth
WAYNE JOHNSTON
ISBN 978–1–897126–35–6

Un art de vivre par temps de catastrophe
DANY LAFERRIÈRE
ISBN 978–0–88864–553–1

The Sasquatch at Home
Traditional Protocols & Modern Storytelling
EDEN ROBINSON
ISBN 978–0–88864–559–3

Imagining Ancient Women
ANNABEL LYON
ISBN 978–0–88864–629–3

Burn It
*On Banning, Burning, and Other Inspired
Responses to Books*
LAWRENCE HILL
coming 2013